NATALIE IMBRUGLIA :
LEFT OF THE MIDDLE

MUSIC ARRANGED BY DEREK JONES. >

UNAUTHORISED REPRODUCTION OF ANY PART OF THIS PUBLICATION BY ANY MEANS INCLUDING PHOTOCOPYING IS AN INFRINGEMENT OF COPYRIGHT. >
MUSIC PROCESSED BY PAUL EWERS MUSIC DESIGN. > PRINTED IN GREAT BRITAIN BY PRINTWISE (HAVERHILL) LIMITED, HAVERHILL, SUFFOLK. >

This publication is not for sale in
the EU and/or Australia
or New Zealand

ISBN 0-7935-9596-7

HAL•LEONARD®
CORPORATION
7777 W. BLUEMOUND RD. P.O. BOX 13819 MILWAUKEE, WI 53213

Visit Hal Leonard Online at
www.halleonard.com

TORN

WORDS & MUSIC > ANNE PREVEN, SCOTT CUTLER & PHIL THORNALLEY

that's what's go-ing on____ no - thing's fine,_ I'm torn._
there's just so ma-ny things____ that I____ can search,_ I'm torn._
that's what's go-ing on____ no - thing's right,_ I'm torn._

CHORUS

____ }
____ } I'm_ all out_ of faith,____ this_ is how_ I feel,_ I'm cold and I____ am shamed
____ } *(See block lyric for final chorus)*

____ ly - ing na - ked on the floor____ il - lu - sion nev - er changed____ in - to some-thing real,

____ wide a - wake and I____ can see_ the per - fect sky_ is torn,_ you're a lit - tle late_

Final chorus:
I'm all out of faith
This is how I feel
I'm cold and I'm ashamed
Bound and broken on the floor.
You're a little late
I'm already torn…
Torn…

BIG MISTAKE > >

WORDS & MUSIC > NATALIE IMBRUGLIA & MARK GOLDENBERG

1. There's no sign— on the gate— and there's mud— on your face,—
(Verses 2 & 3 see block lyric))

— don't you think— it's time we re - in - ves - ti - gate this sit - u - a - tion,

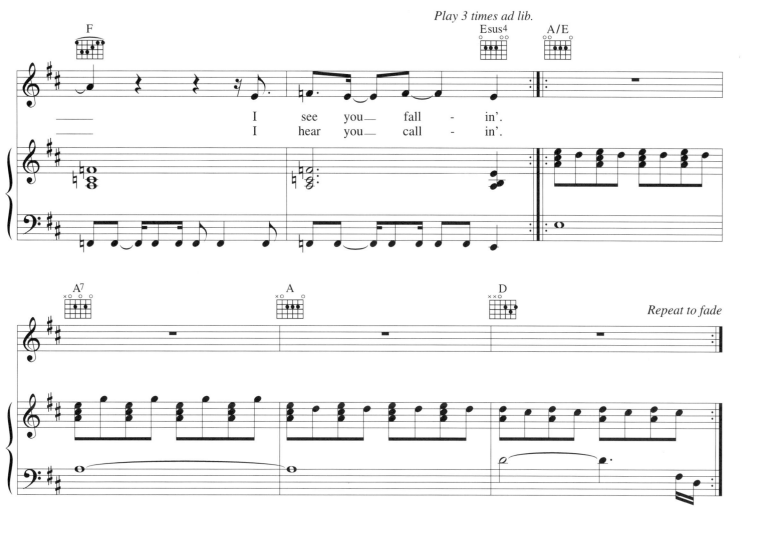

Verse 2:
Got a buzz in my head
And my flowers are dead
Can't figure out a way to rectify this situation
Don't believe what you said.

You forgotten how it started *etc.*

Verse 3:
I could sting like a bee
Careful how you treat me
Baby I don't think I'll accept your sorry invitation
Close the door as you leave.

You forgotten how it started *etc.*

LEAVE ME ALONE > >

WORDS & MUSIC > NATALIE IMBRUGLIA & ANDY WRIGHT

leave me a - lone,__   just leave me a - lone.__

Da de da de da de da de da.

Verse 2:
You like me to stroke you
Careful I don't choke you
Did you read my mind?
You say don't be blue
Is that the best you can do?
I've lost my patience now.

Oh leave me alone *etc.*

INTUITION

WORDS & MUSIC > NATALIE IMBRUGLIA, PHIL THORNALLEY & DAVE MUNDAY

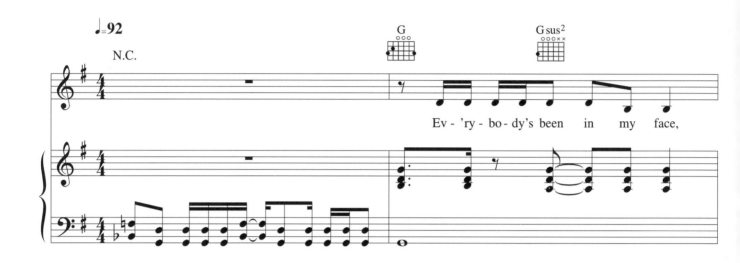

Ev-'ry-bo-dy's been in my face,

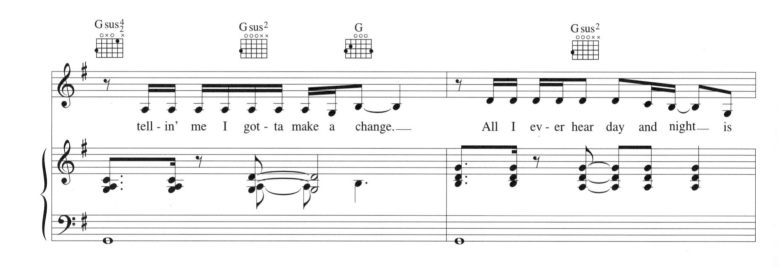

tell-in' me I got-ta make a change.___ All I ev-er hear day and night___ is

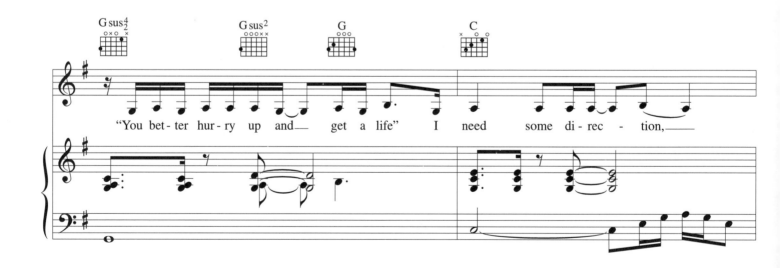

"You bet-ter hur-ry up and___ get a life" I need some di-rec-tion,___

And all I can say is in-tu-i-tion tells me how to live my day. In-tu-i-tion tells me when to walk a-way. Could have turned left, could have turned right, but I end-ed up here bang— in the mid-dle of a re-al life.

Verse 2:
Then another one always says
She'd do anything to get ahead
She doesn't care if she has to scratch
And claw to get in the door
She wants her fifteen minutes of fame
And twenty would be nice
But I guess it's her life.

'Cause intuition tells me that I'm doin' fine
Intuition tells me when to draw the line
Could have turned left, could have turned right
But I ended up here bang in the middle of a real life.

SMOKE > >

WORDS & MUSIC > NATALIE IMBRUGLIA & MATT BRONLEEWEE

1. My lul - la - by hung out to dry,

(Verse 2 see block lyric)

what's up with that? It's ov - er.

Where are you dad? Mum's look-in' sad,

1.

what's up with that? It's dark— in here.

Why__ bleed-ing is__ breath-ing, you're hid-ing

un - der - neath__ the smoke in the room.__ Try,__

Con pedale

Repeat ad lib. to fade

Verse 2:
My mouth is dry
Forgot how to cry
What's up with that?
You're hurting me
I'm running fast
Can't hide the past
What's up with that?

ONE MORE ADDICTION > >

WORDS & MUSIC > NATALIE IMBRUGLIA, PHIL THORNALLEY & DAVE MUNDAY

1. First the good___ news, it's gon-na feel ve-ry nice. Then the bad

(Verse 2 see block lyric)

___ news, you got-ta pay a hea-vy price. Rip tide, we slide, we ride on a

deep for-bid-den sea.___ Un-der we go so slow, and you're hang-ing on___to me.___ And I___ say

Verse 2:
I reject you, but I can't follow through
I'd forget you, but you'd end up tappin' on my back door
Somehow I lost myself in a tunnel long and black
Somewhere at the end, I pretend, there's a way of turning back.

And I say oh, oh one more addiction *etc.*

WORDS & MUSIC > NATALIE IMBRUGLIA & MARK GOLDENBERG

1. Got - ta get___ back,___ got - ta fig - ure out___ a way___
(Verse 2 see block lyric)

Tacet 1°

Don't be-lieve___ a thing___ they say___ to - day.___

Turn a - round___ and walk___ a - way.

Ev - 'ry - thing

Verse 2:
All alone but I'm in a crowded room
I'm sinking in quicksand tonight
You pick me up and I shine across the sky
Till morning, then you colour me in.
Guess it won't amount to much
Seems to me I've lost my touch
I'm back in line
Don't believe a thing they say today
Turn around and walk away
Everything will go your way, I pray
Seems we all get lost amongst the pigeons and the crumbs.

DON'T YOU THINK? > >

WORDS & MUSIC > PHIL THORNALLEY & COLIN CAMPSIE

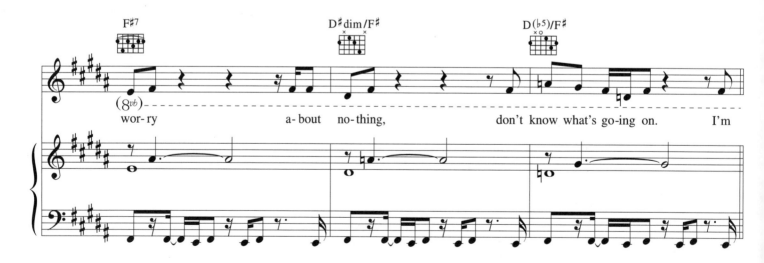

Don't you think,— don't you think, don't you think— that may - be it's

time,— yes it's

time,—

1.

it's time you start - ed think - ing.

Verse 2:
Brother shoots brother
But meanwhile you're fixing up your face
You're not affected by the truth unless it's on your doorstep
Deodorise your paradise, no point in getting crazy.

Don't you think *etc.*

WORDS & MUSIC > NATALIE IMBRUGLIA, RICK PALOMBI & NICK TREVISIK

1. Sweet con-fet-ti out look-ing for a sav-iour,
(Verse 2 see block lyric)

find-ing it hard to break the chain, noth-ing ven-

on his vest,— all that mo-ney you de-serve the best.— I'm im-pressed,—

F#dim   Fmaj7   Esus4   Am

1.

I'm im - pressed,— I'm im - pressed.—

F6   Am   F6

2.

N.C.

Ev - 'ry day— is like— your birth - day,

But the can-dle's burn - ing,_____
don't you_ see, don't you_ see?
Six foot lean-ing on a li - zard chest,_
two red dra - gons ir - oned on his vest,_ all that mo - ney you de -

Verse 2:
What you've got isn't all that you've been given
Changing your body like you change your jeans
Nothing is ever as it seems
Something tells me it's a marriage made in heaven
Stealing your look from a magazine
Playing the part from a movie scene.

Six foot leaning *etc.*

WISHING I WAS THERE > >

WORDS & MUSIC > NATALIE IMBRUGLIA, PHIL THORNALLEY & COLIN CAMPSIE

1. Take your

hand and place it in— my pock-et, flick your eyes back in— their sock-ets.—
(Verse 2 see block lyric)

Verse 2:
I dreamt about another girl in bed with you
You just laughed and smiled, denied the proof
We're fine till I think of a problem
I wish it made sense, like a joke that no one gets
It's a life without regret
I want it to feel that way for ever and ever.

I know I get cold *etc.*

CITY > >

WORDS & MUSIC > NATALIE IMBRUGLIA & PHIL THORNALLEY

1. Had a dream, had a drown - ing dream,— I was in a riv - er of pain.—
(Verses 2 & 3 see block lyric)

On - ly diff - 'rence this time I was - n't call - ing out—— your name, yeah

Verse 2:
Funny how those friends forget you
When you tire of their games
You miss a show or a party that blows
And they've forgotten your name, yeah
And you wonder what you've become
They pull you back when you try to run.

Well anybody heading in my direction *etc.*

Verse 3:
I left the me I used to be
I wanna see this through
I left the me I used to be
If only you'd see it too
Well I wonder what you've become
You pull me back when I try to run.

Well anybody heading in my direction *etc.*

LEFT OF THE MIDDLE > >

WORDS & MUSIC > NATALIE IMBRUGLIA & STEVE BOOKER

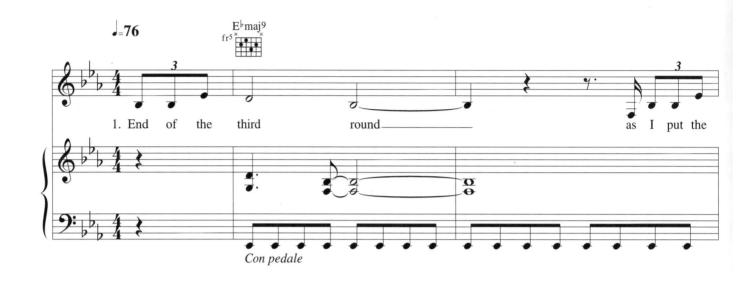

1. End of the third round_____ as I put the

phone down._____ Chas-ing the same lines_____

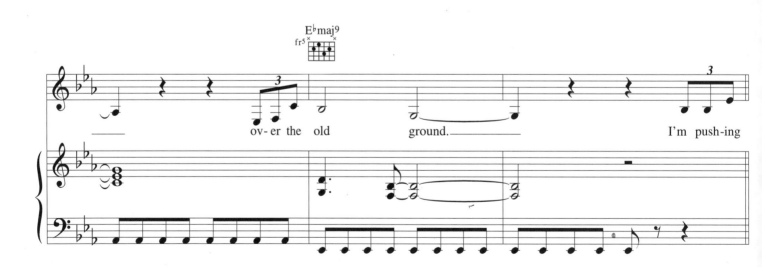

_____ ov-er the old ground._____ I'm push-ing

Verse 2:
I got my ticket and I got a straight road
But I'm passing the same signs over and over.
And my world falls down
And I'm there calling out
But it's something I can't say *etc.*

3/98 (30435)